Second Edition

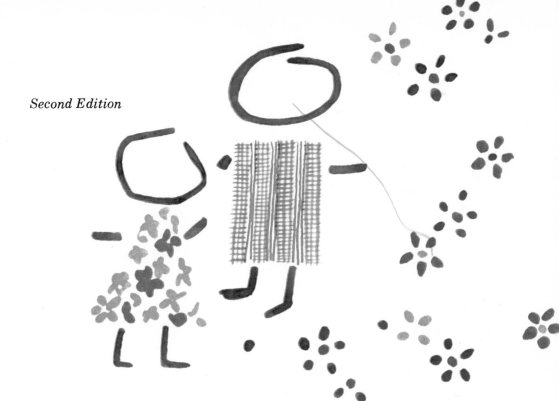

Together
We Go

Stories and articles by *Elizabeth K. Cooper*

 Harcourt Brace Jovanovich, Inc.

New York   Chicago   San Francisco   Atlanta   Dallas

 The Bookmark Reading Program

EARLY   COOPER   SANTEUSANIO   ADELL

Contents

School Days

ISBN 0-15-332185-7

ACKNOWLEDGMENTS: For permission to reprint copyrighted material, grateful acknowledgment is made to the following sources:

ATHENEUM PUBLISHERS, INC.: "A Yell for Yellow" by Eve Merriam, copyright © 1962 by Eve Merriam, from *There Is No Rhyme for Silver*.

GOLDEN PRESS, INC.: Adaptation based on *Too Many Bozos* by Lilian Moore, © copyright 1960 by Golden Press, Inc.

HENRY Z. WALCK, INC. and LOIS LENSKI: "The Sidewalk Is My Yard" from *We Live In The City* by Lois Lenski, copyright, 1954, by Lois Lenski. Published by J. B. Lippincott Company.

Over the Hill and Far Away

From Trees to Paper

City Friends

Too Many Bozos

The artists in this book and the pages on which their work appears are as follows: John Gretzer, pp. 5–62; Manny Haller, pp. 63, 110, 131, 134, 167; Lynn Sweat, pp. 65–109; Allan Mardon, pp. 113–130; Wilson McLean, pp. 133, 135–166; Loring Eutemey, pp. 169–191.

School Days

Going to School

The boy with the lunch box is Ben.
Ben lives in a small house.
He lives far away from the city.
It is morning, and Ben is going
to school.
He rides to school in the bus
that comes up the road.

Ben likes to go to school.
Some days he brings things to school for his friends to see.

Ben's school is small, but the school yard is big.
After lunch, Ben plays in the big yard with his friends.

When school is over for the day, the school bus comes back.
Then Ben rides back to his house.

This girl is Penny.

Penny lives in a tall apartment building in the city.

She is going to a big city school.

The school is not far from Penny's apartment building.

Penny is with her friend Ted.

Ted lives in the apartment building down the street from Penny.

Penny and Ted walk to school.

When they get to school, they
play in the school yard.

The school yard is small for
a big school.

Penny and Ted do not bring lunch
boxes to school.

Penny walks back to her apartment for
lunch, but Ted eats the school lunch.

Is the school that Penny and Ted
go to like Ben's school?

A Surprise at School

A bus came down the road.
It was filled with boys and girls.

Soon the bus was in the school yard.
The children got down from the bus.
They ran into the school building.
All but Ben, that is.
Ben still sat in the bus.

10

"Good morning," said the teacher
as the children walked in.

"Good morning," said the children.

The teacher looked at the children.
She did not see Ben.
"Was Ben on the bus?" she asked.

"Yes," said all the children.

"He had a big box," Wendy said.

"Wendy, go and see what Ben is
up to," said the teacher.

Wendy ran back to the school yard.
Ben was pulling the box up the walk.

"Wendy," Ben said, "come and help.
Help me bring this box to the room!"

Wendy ran to Ben.
"What is it?" she asked.

"A surprise for the room," Ben said.
Wendy and Ben picked up the box
and went into the school building.

The teacher looked at the box as
Ben and Wendy came into the room.

"What in the world is that?"
the teacher asked.
She went over and looked in the box.
She was surprised!

"Can we see it?" asked the children
as they jumped up.

"You must sit down," said the teacher.
"Then Ben will let all of you see it."
The children sat down fast, and Ben
got the surprise from the box.

The surprise was a big turtle.
"See!" Ben said. "Dad got it for me.
Dad said that turtles make good pets."

Ben put the turtle down and said,
"All you can see now is the shell.
The turtle lives in the shell."

"I wish we had the turtle for a pet,"
said a girl.

"Do all of you wish we had it for
a pet?" asked the teacher.

"Yes, yes," said the happy children.
And so, Ben's room had a pet.

Turtles

Ben's turtle came from a turtle egg.
All turtles hatch from eggs.

When the turtle eggs hatch, the
little turtles are hungry.
But the mother turtle will not bring
her little turtles things to eat.
The little turtles must look for
what they need.

A turtle's legs are very little.
Its legs are so small that it
can't walk very fast.
It can't run at all.

But turtles do not need to go fast.
When something runs after a turtle,
it just pulls back into its shell.
Then its big shell is all you can see.

You can pick up a turtle.
You can look at its legs and shell.
When you pick a turtle up fast,
what do you think it will do?

Ben's pet turtle was not from a pond.
It was a turtle that lives on land.
It was a land turtle.

Some land turtles live on land
that gets very little rain.
They do not need a pond.
They do not need to get wet.
And they do not need water to drink.
They get all the water they need
from the things they eat.

All turtles are not land turtles.
Some of them are pond turtles.
Pond turtles live around ponds.
They need water.

Pond turtles can go down, down
into the water.
But soon they must come back up.

When pond turtles are on land,
they can't go fast.
But when they get into water,
just look at them go.

Turtles make good pets.

You can just put a pet land turtle in a box.

A pet land turtle will not need water, but it will need things to eat.

But pond turtles will need some water.

You must not forget the water when you get a pond turtle for a pet.

All pet turtles are fun to look at.

Children can play with them and bring them things to eat.

Turtles make good pets for the room at school.

Land Turtle

Pond Turtle

Painting Day

Fog was over the city, and a
light rain came down.

It was a cold, winter afternoon.

The boys and girls had just come
back to the room after lunch.

Some children walked into the room with wet umbrellas and wet hats.

They put them away and sat down.

"This is a good afternoon to paint," said Mr. Grant.

"I think I will let you paint a big picture for the room."

"Can we paint a bright picture?" asked a girl.

"Yes," Mr. Grant said, "a bright picture is good for this dark day.

Now, what colors will we need?"

"We need blue for the sky," said Ted.

"Yellow for the sun," said his friend.

"And red for the flowers," said Penny.

"Green for the grass," said her friend.

"And black for the clouds," said Ted.

"Black is not a good color for a bright picture," said Penny.

"Then I will paint the sky all blue," said Ted.

Mr. Grant looked for the paints.
He had yellow, black, red, and blue.
But he had no green.

"What a funny thing," he said.
"Did I forget the green paint?
I will get some as you are painting.
You can paint the green things last."

The children painted cars and trucks.
They painted flowers and gardens.
They painted rockets and planes.
They painted big and little people.

Penny got the yellow paint.
She painted a bright, yellow sun.

Ted got the blue paint.
He painted a blue sky.
As Ted painted, he got some blue
paint on Penny's yellow sun.
What a surprise!
The blue paint on the yellow sun
made the sun green!

"Look, Mr. Grant," said Penny.
"We do not need green paint.
We can make a green color with
yellow and blue."

And so they did.
They put some blue paint into a jar.
Then they put in some yellow paint.

"Now shake it," said Mr. Grant.
Soon the jar was filled with
green paint.

The children painted the green grass.
They painted a car and a house green.
They painted green things all over
the big picture.

At last Ted made a duck in a pond.
What color do you think he painted
the water?

Color Magic

The world is filled with colors
Colors are all around you.

Look for them in the room.
Do you see something red?
Do you see something yellow?
Do you see something blue?
Do you see other colors?
What other colors do you see?

It is fun to paint with bright colors.
Red, yellow, and blue are like magic.
With them, you can make other colors.

You can mix yellow paint with
blue paint.
What color will you get?

Next, you can mix yellow paint
with red paint.
What color do you think you will get?

You can mix red paint with blue paint.
Now what color will you get?

Some colors are light.
Other colors are dark.
What light green things do you see?
What dark green things do you see?

You can make light green paint.
Just put a little yellow paint into
some dark green paint.
As you mix in the yellow paint,
you will get light green paint.

Next, you can make dark green.
Just put a little blue paint into
some light green paint.

The world is filled with colors.
They are all around you.
Of all the colors you see, what color
do you like best?
Can you make the color you like best?

Do you think colors are like magic?
What makes them like magic?

A Yell for Yellow

Yellow, yellow, hello, yellow—
Welcome to forsythia and dandelions
   in Spring,
To buttercups and goldenrod and
   warblers on the wing.

Yellow, yellow, mellow yellow—
Yellow as new wood, yellow as wheat,
Yellow as cornbread sweet to eat.

Yellow, yellow, let's bellow yellow—
Yellow monkeys peeling bananas!
Yellow chickens playing pianos!
Butterflies, goldfish, cats' eyes!

Yellow, yellow, yell on yellow—
Yellow is a lemon smell, it tingles
   like a sneeze,
Tickles like the sunshine, jingles
   like a breeze!

EVE MERRIAM

A Frog in School

The children in Miss Lester's
room liked to sing songs.

"Can we sing a song this morning?"
asked a girl in a yellow dress.

"Yes," said Miss Lester, "I made up
a song as I came to school.
I will sing it for you."

This was the song that Miss Lester
had made up.

"Hop!" said the big frog.
"Hop!" said the little frog.
"Hop to the pond in the park."
"Splash!" said the big frog.
"Splash!" said the little frog.
"Splash in the pond in the park."

"Jump!" said the big frog.
"Jump!" said the little frog.
"Jump in the light of the moon."
"Dance!" said the big frog.
"Dance!" said the little frog.
"Dance in the light of the moon."

Greg's hand went up.
"I can make up a frog dance to go with the song," he said.

"Good," said Miss Lester.
"Some of you can dance with Greg.
And others can sing with me."

What a funny dance!
Greg put his hands down and jumped around like a frog.
Some children danced with Greg.
Other children helped Miss Lester with the singing.

As Greg danced around the room,
he got a surprise.

He looked down at a big green frog!

The frog was jumping around the room
with the children.

"Look, Miss Lester!" yelled Greg.

"A frog jumped into the room."

"We must not yell," said Miss Lester.

"Think of my poor ears."

She put her hands over her ears and
went on singing.

Just then, the big green frog jumped
over next to the teacher's chair.
  Miss Lester looked down at last.

  "Help! A frog is in the room!"
yelled Miss Lester.
  "Did you bring that frog in, Greg?"

  "No," said Greg. "It just came in.
It came to help with the frog dance."

  "Good for him," said Miss Lester as
she went back to her chair.
  "We need all the help we can get.
Come on. Away we go!"

Miss Lester and some of the children went on singing.

As other children danced, the frog was all over the room.

When it was all over, Miss Lester asked, "What did you like best?"

"The frog," yelled the children. "We liked the frog best of all."

"Did you like the song?" asked Miss Lester.

All the hands went up, and Miss Lester was happy.

Frogs

Now Miss Lester's room has a pet.
The pet frog came from a pond.
It swam in the pond, and then it
jumped up to the land.
It came down the road and into
Miss Lester's room.

A frog will not go very far from water.
It likes to stay wet.
It can go far down into the water,
but it can't stay down.
A frog has to come back up.

Frogs can't stay far away from water.
They must go to the water to lay eggs.
The eggs they lay are very small.

Tadpoles come from frog eggs.
Tadpoles are not like frogs.
The tadpoles stay down in the water.
They do not need to come up.

Tadpoles do not look like frogs.
A frog has big legs.
But a little tadpole has no legs.
It can't run. It can't jump.
What can a tadpole do?

A tadpole has to stay in water.
It eats green things that live in ponds.
The tadpole eats and eats.

Then the tadpole gets legs.
And at last the day comes when it
can live on land.
Then it is a little frog.

The little frog can stay on land
and hop in the grass.
The little frog looks for bugs to eat.
It eats and eats and eats.
At last it is a big frog.

The Peter Rabbit Play

Jeff jumped from his bed.

This was the day for the Peter Rabbit play at school.

And Jeff's teacher was going to let him play Peter Rabbit.

Jeff dressed very fast that morning.
He got something to eat.
Then he ran from his apartment.
Soon he was at school with all the
other boys and girls.

"Boys and girls," said the teacher.
"You won't forget what to do in
the play, will you?
Jeff, what are you in the play?"

"I won't forget," said Jeff.

"I am Peter Rabbit, and I am bad.
I run away from the rabbit house.
I get hungry, and so I go into
Mr. McGregor's garden.
I eat and eat and eat."

"What comes next?" said the teacher.

Billy's hand went up.
"I run after Peter Rabbit," he said.
"I am Mr. McGregor, and I yell at him.
I don't like rabbits eating things in
my garden."

"Then what?" said the teacher.

"I jump into a big can," said Jeff.
"But the can has water in it, and
I get all wet.
So I jump from the can when
Mr. McGregor is not looking.
He won't get his hands on me!
I run away as fast as my legs can go."

"And then?" said the teacher.

"I go back to my mother," said Jeff.
"And my mother gets after me.
And, boy, do I get it from her!"

"I am the mother," said a tall girl.

"Peter was very bad.

He has to go to bed hungry.

The other rabbits get something to eat, but not poor Peter.

Bad rabbits must go to bed hungry."

"Very good," said the teacher.

"Now, rabbits, get the ears and put them on."

The children went to a box and got the rabbit ears they had made.

The teacher looked at the children.

"Billy," she said, "are you a little mixed up?

You are the man, Mr. McGregor.

You don't need rabbit ears."

"What am I thinking of!" said Billy.

He put the ears back in the box.

Then the children from the next room came to see the play.

The play was good, and the children liked it.

It was fun when Peter hid in the can.

It was fun when Mr. McGregor yelled.

But the best fun of all came when Mr. McGregor put on rabbit ears.

The Little Red Hen

This is a play for you to do.
You will need children to play

The Little Red Hen
The Duck
The Mouse
The Rabbit

RED HEN: This is my bag of wheat seeds.
   I must plant them in my garden.
   But I need help.
   Will you help me plant the wheat?

DUCK: Not I! I am looking for bugs.

MOUSE: Not I! I can't get up.

RABBIT: Not I! I must go to sleep.

RED HEN: Then I will plant it myself.

BOYS: And so she did.

A GIRL: Little Red Hen dug up her
garden and planted the wheat.
Soon wheat came up in her garden.

RED HEN: Now the summer is over.
And now the wheat is yellow.
I must cut my yellow wheat.
But I need help.
Will you help me cut the wheat?

DUCK: Not I! I must go to the city.

MOUSE: Not I! I can't stay in the sun.

RABBIT: Not I! I don't like to cut wheat.

RED HEN: Then I will cut it myself.

GIRLS: And so she did.

48

A BOY: Little Red Hen cut the wheat.
Then she put the wheat in bags.
She filled all the bags with wheat.

RED HEN: I must make the wheat into
good, rich flour.
But I need help.
Will you help me make the flour?

DUCK: Not I! I must look for my hat.

MOUSE: Not I! I must go to the park.

RABBIT: Not I! I can't make flour.

RED HEN: Then I will make it myself.

BOYS: And so she did.

49

A GIRL: Little Red Hen made the wheat into flour.

RED HEN: Look at my good, rich flour!
I will make a cake with this flour.
But I need help.
Will you help make the cake?

DUCK: Not I! I must get some water.

MOUSE: Not I! I am going to a party.

RABBIT: Not I! I can't make a cake.

RED HEN: Then I will make it myself.

GIRLS: And so she did.

50

A GIRL: Little Red Hen made
the cake. It was the best cake in
the world.

RED HEN: I made this big yellow cake.
Will you help me eat the cake?

DUCK: I will!

MOUSE: I will!

RABBIT: I will!

RED HEN: No, you won't help!
I planted the wheat seeds myself.
I cut the yellow wheat myself.
I made the wheat into flour.
And then I made this cake.
You did not help me then.
So you won't help me now.
I will eat all the cake myself!

ALL: And so she did.

A Walk Around the School

"Boys and girls, this morning we will go for a walk," said the teacher.

"We won't go far.

We will just walk around the school and look for things that are moving.

Look for moving things in the grass.

Look for moving things in the sky.

We will tell about the things we see."

The children went from the building and walked about the yard.

They looked up at the blue sky.

They looked down at the green grass.

At last they all sat down.

"Now tell me about the moving things you see," said the teacher.

"I see some ants that are moving," said a girl.

"And a red bug is moving up a plant."

A boy lay back on the grass.

"I see clouds," he said.

"They are moving fast in the sky."

"I see a bird," yelled a boy.
"It just came from its nest."

"What do you think is in the nest?"
the teacher asked.

"Little birds," said the boy.

"Eggs," said other children.

"Yes," said the teacher, "I think the
nest has eggs in it.
We must stay away from it and
let the bird come back.
It sits on the eggs so they will hatch.
What will come from the eggs when
they hatch?"

"Little birds," yelled the children.

Soon the bird came back.
"See its colors," said the teacher.
"The bird looks black in the shadows.
But in the sun you can see bright
colors on its back."

As the children looked, the bird went
up to its nest.

"Children, look at that," the teacher
said as she looked at a tall plant.

"Look at the web," said the teacher.
"See the spider moving over the web."

"I don't like spiders," said a girl.

"I do," said the boy next to her.
"We need spiders in this world."

"I don't need them," said the girl.

"Yes, you do," said the boy.

"Now, children," said the teacher.
"The best thing to do is to go
back to the room.
Then we can look up things
about spiders."

56

Spider Webs

Spiders eat bugs.

They spin webs to get the bugs
they need to eat.

Some spiders make webs in gardens.

Some spiders make webs in the grass.

Some spiders make webs in houses.

Look at the web in this picture.
Look at the spider that made the web.
It is a garden spider.

The web of a garden spider looks
like a little net.

When a bug lands in the net, it
won't get out.

It can shake the web, but it can't
get out.

When the web shakes, the garden
spider runs to the bug.

The hungry spider eats the bug.

The web in this picture looks
something like a small bag.

It is the web of a grass spider.

First the grass spider spins its web.
Then it sits under the web.
Bugs that run in the grass don't
see the web.

And they can't see the hungry spider
that sits under the web.

The bugs land in the web, and down
they go!

Do you think they get out?

Flower spiders live in flowers.

When you first look at a flower, you will not see the spider.

Flower spiders are very small and very light in color.

The small bugs that come to the flower don't see the flower spider.

But the flower spider sees the bugs.

Then the spider has something to eat.

House spiders spin webs in the house.
Mothers do not like to see spider
webs in the house.
But spiders are a help to us.
They help us when they eat some
of the bugs that are bad for people.
It is good that spiders eat bugs.

---

1. What do hungry spiders eat?

2. Do the webs of garden spiders look
   like the webs of grass spiders?

How Many Legs?

How many legs has a robin?
  A robin has two,
  And it hops in the sun.
How many legs has a rabbit?
  A rabbit has four
  To jump and to run.

How many legs has a cricket?
  A cricket has six
  For jumping and hopping.
How many legs has a spider?
  A spider has eight
  To run without stopping.

How many legs has a crab?
  Some crabs have ten!
  A crab is not slow.
How many legs has a snake?
  A snake has none,
  But look at it go!

ELIZABETH K. COOPER

62

Can You Read This?

Linda came into her room with a big pan of water.

She set the pan on the rug.

Then she got her fish and put all six of them in the pan.

Just then Linda's cat came in.

She sat on the rug, looking at the six fish.

"No, you don't," said Linda.

"You are not going to eat my fish."

At that, Linda picked up the cat and took her to the yard.

Thinking Back

What did the story tell you?

Linda did not like her cat.
Cats like to eat fish.

New Ways with Words

Did you know all the words in the story?
Can you read the words in the box now?

pan	six	took
set	rug	fish

How did the picture help you?
How did other words in the sentence help you?

Try This

This sentence has a new word in it.

Jan put on her hat and coat.

What did Jan put on?

Over the Hill and Far Away

The Big Race

"I will race you up that big hill,"
said a rabbit when he met a turtle.

"I can't race," said the turtle.
"Look at my funny legs.
Look at my big shell.
I can't run fast at all."

"Come on," said the rabbit.

"I will do my best," said the turtle.

At that, the rabbit's ears went back.
He got set for the race.

"We will race up the road to the top of the hill," he said.

"Are you all set, Turtle?"

The turtle got his little legs out from under his big shell.

"All set," he said.

"Then go!" yelled the rabbit.

The rabbit ran like lightning.
The turtle walked, but not very fast.
The big race was on.

It was a bright summer day,
and the sun was hot.

The rabbit ran fast up the road.

He looked back, but he did not
see the turtle.

"I don't need to go so fast," said
the rabbit.

"That poor little turtle can't get
to the top of the hill first.

I am so hot, I think I will stop."

So the rabbit sat down under a tree.
Soon he went to sleep.

The turtle just walked on and on.
He went as fast as a turtle can go,
and that is not very fast.
But he did not stop.

At last the turtle came to the
rabbit under the tree.
The rabbit was sleeping, but the
turtle did not stop.
The turtle just went on up the hill.
And at last he came to the top.

When the rabbit jumped up, the sun
was far down in the sky.

"What a good sleep I had!" he said.
"Now I must run to the top of the
hill, and get this race over with."

When the rabbit came to the top,
he had a surprise.
The turtle sat on top of the hill!

"You can run fast, my friend,"
said the turtle.
"You can run fast, but you still
lost the race.
To come in first, you must not stop.
You must go on and on and on."

The Lion and the Mouse

A happy little mouse ran in the hot morning sun.

He raced up and down the hills.

He jumped over little rocks.

He ran around big rocks.

And then he ran into the tall grass.

The grass was so tall that the poor little mouse got lost.

At last the mouse had to stop.

A dark shadow was all around him.

The little mouse looked around to
see what made the dark shadow.

It was not a big tree.

It was not a big rock.

It was a big lion!

The lion picked up the mouse.

"Now you won't get away,"
the lion said.

The poor mouse looked at the lion.
His ears and legs began to shake.

"Let me go! Let me go!" he yelled.
He began to pull to get away.

"It will do you no good to shake
and pull," said the lion.
"I am going to eat you."

The poor mouse looked up at the lion.
"Let me go," he said, "and I will do
something good for you.
Some day you will need my help."

"That is very funny!" said the lion.
"What can you do to help me?
I am the king! A king needs no help.
But what you said is so funny, I will
let you go."

The lion let the mouse go, and the
mouse fell into the grass.
In a flash, the mouse jumped up.
Then away he ran, as fast as a little
mouse can go.

That afternoon, the mouse began
to look for seeds to eat.

He ran far, and then something
made him stop.

"That is my friend, the lion!" he said.

"I think he needs help.

But where is he?"

The mouse began to look for the lion.

He ran to the top of the hill, where
the lion was in a net.

"Help! Help!" yelled the lion.

"I fell into this big net and now
I can't get out."

The little mouse went to the net.
First, he pulled at the big net.
Next, he bit into it.
He bit and bit and bit.
And at last the net let go.

The big lion looked down at his good
little friend.
"You did not forget me," he said.
"A little mouse like you can help a
big lion like me after all."

Chicken Little

This is a play for you to do.
You will need children to play

    Chicken Little
    Henny Penny
    Ducky Lucky
    Turkey Lurkey
    Foxy Loxy

CHICKEN LITTLE: I am Chicken Little.
I live in this house.
This is the yard around it.
I am under a tree in my yard.
But what was that?
Something fell on my back.
I think it was the sky!
I must run and tell the king.

A BOY: Chicken Little began to run.
Soon she met Henny Penny.

HENNY PENNY: Chicken Little,
where are you going?

CHICKEN LITTLE: I am going to tell the
king that the sky is falling.

HENNY PENNY: Where did it fall?

CHICKEN LITTLE: On me! So I must
tell the king!

HENNY PENNY: Then I will go with you.

A GIRL: Henny Penny ran down the
road with Chicken Little.
Soon they met Ducky Lucky.

DUCKY LUCKY: Where are you going,
Chicken Little and Henny Penny?

HENNY PENNY: We are going to tell the
king that the sky is falling.

DUCKY LUCKY: Did you see it fall?

HENNY PENNY: No, but Chicken Little
said that some of it fell on her.

DUCKY LUCKY: Then I must go with you.

A BOY: Away they went down the road.
Soon they came to Turkey Lurkey.

TURKEY LURKEY: Where are you going, my good friends?

DUCKY LUCKY: We are going to tell the king that the sky is falling!

TURKEY LURKEY: Where did it fall?

DUCKY LUCKY: It fell on Chicken Little.

TURKEY LURKEY: Then we must tell the king.

A GIRL: Turkey Lurkey ran with Chicken Little and her friends. Soon they met Foxy Loxy.

FOXY LOXY: Stop! Stop!
Where are you going so fast?

TURKEY LURKEY: We must see the king.
The sky is falling.

FOXY LOXY: What! The sky is falling!

TURKEY LURKEY: A bit of it fell on
Chicken Little.

FOXY LOXY: Come with me.
You can stay at my house.
And I will tell the king.

CHICKEN LITTLE: No, you won't!
You will eat us all.
Help! Run!

A BOY: Away ran Chicken Little and
her friends.
They ran to Chicken Little's house.
Foxy Loxy ran after them, but they
did not let him in.

CHICKEN LITTLE: We can come out now.
Foxy Loxy has run away.
He will not eat us this day!

A GIRL: Just then something fell
from Chicken Little's back.
Chicken Little picked it up.

CHICKEN LITTLE: What is this?
Is this what fell on me?
It is not the sky at all.
It is just something that
fell from the tree.

HENNY PENNY: Then the sky
is not falling after all!

DUCKY LUCKY: And we don't
need to tell the king!

A Father, His Boy,
and the Donkey

A father and his boy had a little donkey that was not very good.

The day had come for them to plant some wheat.

But they had no wheat seeds.

"We must trade the donkey for some seeds," said the father.

So they set out to make the trade.

On the road to the city, the father
and his boy met some children.

"Look at them!" said a girl.

"The father has a donkey, but he
makes his little boy walk!"

The father said, "Then I'll let
the boy ride.
Donkeys are made to ride on."

So he put the boy on the donkey.
They went on down the road to trade
the little donkey.

Soon they met a little old woman.

"I'm surprised at that boy," the old woman said.

"He rides the donkey and makes his poor old father walk!"

At that, the boy said, "Stop, Father. I'm going to let you ride."

And the boy got down from the donkey and helped his father up.

They went on down the road.
Soon they met some other people.

"Where is that big man going on that poor little donkey?" asked a man.
"I'm surprised they don't let the poor donkey ride on the man."

So the father jumped down and picked up the little donkey.
The boy helped, and they put the donkey on the father's back.
They walked on down the road.

At last, they came to a hill.

"Not so fast!" said the father.

"I can't walk fast with this donkey on my back."

Just then the father fell over a rock.

Down he went with the donkey on top of him.

The boy ran to help his father.

"What a day!" the father said.

"From now on, I won't let people tell me what to do.

I'll just do what I think is best."

The Bremen Band

A man had a very old donkey.

The donkey was so old that he was no good at all on the man's farm.

So the man sent the donkey away, out into the cold world.

The donkey was sad and hungry as he began to walk away from the farm.

The donkey did not go far when
he met a dog.

"Where are you going?" asked the dog.

"I was sent away from the farm,"
said the donkey.

"So I'm going to Bremen to play
in the band.

Will you come with me?"

The dog, like the donkey, was hungry.
So he said, "Yes, I'll go with you.
Then we can get something to eat."

And the dog went down the road
with the donkey.

Soon they met a cat.

"Let me tell you something sad,"
said the cat.

"The rich man I lived with sent
me away."

"It was like that with us," said
the donkey.

"So we are going to Bremen
to play in the band."

"Then I'll go with you," said the cat.
And he went down the road with the
dog and the donkey.

They came to a farm where a rooster hid under a rock.

"What are you doing under that rock?" asked the donkey.

"A man is looking for me," said the rooster.

"He said he is going to eat me."

"You must get away from this farm," said the donkey.

"Come to Bremen with us and play in the band."

So the rooster went with the donkey and his friends.

The House Under the Trees

The friends walked all day.

After the sun went down, the stars and the moon came out.

The friends walked on in the bright moonlight.

At last they came to a house under some trees.

The donkey went to the house.
"It looks like a rich house," he said.

"What do you see?" asked the cat.

"I see the kitchen," said the donkey.
"I see hot things to eat and cold
milk to drink.
The people in the kitchen are robbers!
The robbers are all set to eat.
Can we get them out of the house?"

"I'll tell you what to do," said
the rooster.

The friends did what the rooster said.

First, the dog jumped up on top of the donkey.

Next, the cat jumped up on the dog. Last, the rooster jumped up on the cat.

"Let us make the robbers run away," said the rooster. "Get set! Go!"

At that, the band began.

The donkey went "Hee-haw, hee-haw."

The dog went, "Bow-wow, bow-wow."

The cat went, "Me-ow, me-ow, me-ow."

The rooster went, "Cock-a-doodle-doo, cock-a-doodle-doo, cock-a-doodle-doo."

The robbers jumped up.

Something was after them!

They ran from the house to the hills far away.

After that, the donkey and his friends had a house to live in.

They had a kitchen filled with good things to eat.

They did not go to Bremen after all.

The Little Clay House

A man was going to the city with some bright clay jars.

As he went down the road, he lost his best jar.

The jar fell into the tall grass.

The man did not see the jar fall, and so he did not stop.

He went on down the road.

A little gray mouse ran up to the jar.
He looked at the clay jar and said,
"This looks like a little clay house.
I'll see who lives in it."

The gray mouse looked into the jar.
"Who is in this little jar?" he asked.

All was still, and so the little gray
mouse went in.

"This jar will make a good little house
for me," he said.

The next day, a green frog came over
the grass with a hop, hop, hop.
He came to the clay jar.

"This jar looks like a little clay
house," he said.
"I'll rap on it and see who is in."

And he did. He said,
"Little clay jar, little clay jar!
Who is in this little clay jar?"

"I am !" said the little gray mouse.
"I am in my little clay house.
Who are you?"

"I'm the green frog from the pond.
Will you let me in?" said the frog.

"Come in, come in," said the mouse.
"Come live with me in my house."

The frog came in and looked around.
"I like this house," he said.

That afternoon, a small red hen
came down the road.
She came to the jar that lay in
the tall grass.

"A little house," she said.
"I will rap and see who is in."

And she did. She said,
"Little clay house, little clay house!
Who is in this little clay house?"

"I am!" said the green frog.

"I am!" said the little gray mouse.
"I am in my little clay house.
But who are you?"

"I'm the red hen from the hen yard.
Will you let me come in?" she said.

"Come in, come in," said the mouse.
"You can live in this little clay house."

The hen came in and looked around.
"I think I will stay," she said.

"Good," said the little gray mouse.
"I am happy you came to my house."

The Big Black Bear

The next morning a big black bear
came down from the hills.

He came over to the jar in the grass.

"What a funny jar," said the bear.
"I think I'll see who is in."
And the bear began to rap on the jar.

The bear cried out,
"Little clay house, little clay house!
Who is in this little clay house?"

"I am!" said the green frog.

"I am!" said the red hen.

"I am!" said the little gray mouse.
"I am in my little clay house.
But who are you?"

"I am the big black bear from the far
hills," said the bear. "Let me in!"

"Not you, not you," cried the mouse.
"No bear can live in my house."

The bear cried out,
"I will get you, little mouse.
I'll get you out of that little house!"

The big bear jumped up and came
down on the little clay house.

"Run fast!" cried the little gray mouse.

The hen jumped fast and ran back
to her hen yard.
The frog, with big hops, went back
to his pond.
And the little gray mouse ran away
and hid in the grass.

The clay house was in bits.
The bear sat on the bits of clay.

"Oh! Oh! Oh!" cried the big bear.
"I cut my legs.
And I cut myself where I sit down.
Come back and help me! Come back!"

But the little mouse was far away.
And so was the frog, and so was
the hen.

For days the big black bear cried
when he sat down.
That bad old bear!

Over in the Garden

Over in the garden
In the bright hot sun,
Lived a big mother turtle
And her little turtle one.
"Sleep," said the mother.
"I will sleep," said the one.
"I will sleep all day
In the bright, hot sun."

Over in the garden
Where the pond is blue,
Lived a big mother frog
And her little frogs two.
"Splash," said the mother.
"We will splash," said the two.
"We will splash all day
Where the pond is blue."

Over in the garden
In a tall green tree,
Lived a big mother bird
And her little birds three.
"Sing," said the mother.
"We will sing," said the three.
"We will sing all day
In the tall green tree."

Over in the garden
Where children played before,
Lived a big mother rabbit
And her little rabbits four.
"Hop," said the mother.
"We will hop," said the four.
"We will hop all day
Where children played before."

Over in the garden
In a big beehive,
Lived a big mother bee
And her little bees five.
"Buzz," said the mother.
"We will buzz," said the five.
"We will buzz all day
In the big beehive."

Over in the garden
Where sun and shadow mix,
Lived a big mother duck
And her little ducks six.
"Quack," said the mother.
"We will quack," said the six.
"We will quack all day
Where sun and shadow mix."
Adapted by ELIZABETH K. COOPER

Can You Read This?

Just as Bill looked up, something fell from the tree.

Bill ran to the spot where it fell. He bent down and picked it up.

"You are such a little thing," Bill said as he looked at its little wings.

"I'll put you back in the nest so a cat won't catch you."

Thinking Back

What is the story about?

a little bird

a green tree

Where do you think the nest was?

in the grass

in the tree

New Ways with Words

Some words in the story may be new to you.

How did the story help you to figure out the new words?

Can you read the words now?

spot	bent	wings
such	catch	

What word fits each sentence?

The bird had little w_____.
The bird had little l_____.

Why did you choose **wings** for the first sentence and **legs** for the other one?

Working with Words

Another way to figure out new words is to sound them out.

To sound out a word, you put together the sounds that the letters stand for.

Try This
Try to sound out the words in the box.

sick	chop	ham
shut	beg	

From Trees to Paper

What Is It?

It began as a tree.
Then the tree was cut down.
But now it is not a tree at all.

You can see it in your room at school.
You can see it in your house.
It comes in many colors, and it
is good for many things.

Many things are made of it.
Party hats and toy planes are
made of it.
Pictures are painted on it.
You can put it around a box.
You can cut it into small bits.

You can see it in this book.
And it is in all your other books.
Can you tell what it is before
you look at the next picture?

Now look at the picture.

What are all the things in the
picture made of?

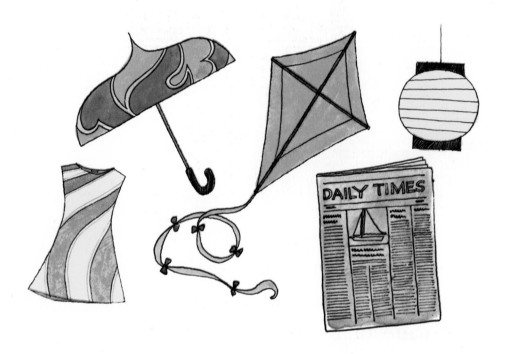

The five things in the picture are
all made of paper.

Are you surprised at some of them?

What do you think of the paper dress
and the bright paper umbrella?

Can you think of other things that
are made of paper?

The first people who lived in this
world did not have paper.

People then did not have many
of the things we have now.

Did they have books to look at?

Did they have paper to paint on?

Did they have paper bags and boxes?

What are the best paper things in
the world?

Some people think books are the best.

What do you think?

Paper Nests

People made the paper in this book.
People made the paper you paint on.
They made all the other paper in
your room.

But people did not make the first
paper in the world.
Wasps made paper before people did.
Wasps made paper from wood.

Wasps build nests with the paper they make.

Look at the picture to see the paper nest of the wasp.

Before a wasp can make a nest, it has to make paper.

It gets a bit of old wood and chews it.

The wasp chews the wood to make it soft and wet.

It chews and chews and chews.

The soft, wet wood is then wood pulp.
With the soft wood pulp, the wasp
builds its nest.

Its nest will have many little rooms.
The rooms are for the wasp's eggs.
When the nest is made, it looks
like paper.

It is paper! It is soft paper that
a wasp made.

Wasps made paper from wood long
before people did.

At first, people did not make paper
from wood at all.

They made paper from grasses and
other things.

Then, long after that, they began
to make paper from wood.

Trees, Pulp, and Paper

Look at the picture.

The trees make you think of wood, don't they?

And now wood makes you think of paper.

The big trees are cut down.
They are then cut into many logs.

The logs are put on long trucks.
They go on the trucks to a pulp mill.

At the pulp mill, the logs are cut
into very small bits of wood.

The bits of wood are then mixed with
very hot water and many other things.

The wood gets very soft.

Before long, it is wood pulp.

The wood pulp is sent to a
paper mill.

At the paper mill, the pulp is
made into paper.

From the paper mill, the paper
comes to us.

A Picture Book

You can make many things
from paper.

One good thing to make from
paper is a picture book.

Get some sheets of paper.
Put the sheets of paper together.
When the sheets are together, make
them into a book like this.

You will need a name for your book.
The name of your book will tell
what it is about.

Will you make a book about the tall
buildings in the city?
Will you make it about a farm?
Will it tell about rockets and planes?
Will it tell about the fun you have
in winter?
What about a book on clouds, rain,
snow, and fog?

A book about a day in the park is
fun to make.
So is a book about your pets.

128

Make two lines on the first sheet
of your book.

Write the name of your book on
the first line.

Then write your name on the next
line, under the name of the book.

Your name will tell who made
the book.

Will you write the names in
bright colors?

Write in the color you like best.

Next, you will need some pictures
for your book.

Paint pictures on all the sheets.
Make the pictures big and bright.

After you paint the first picture, make
some lines under it.

Then write something about the
picture on the lines you made.

Write something about all the pictures
in your book.

Your teacher and your friends will
like to see what you write.

Billy likes to ride.
He rides in my car.

Billy plays in the pond.
He likes the cold water.

Can You Read This?

Stan had just painted a picture.
He had painted it with watercolors.

It was a picture of a bluebird going into a birdhouse.

"Someday I'll surprise Mom with my picture," Stan said to himself.

"But now I'll just put it somewhere in my bedroom."

Thinking Back

What are watercolors?

> something to paint with
> something to drink

What is a bedroom?

> a room to eat in
> a room to sleep in

New Ways with Words

Some words are made by putting together two words.

These words are **compound words**.

Can you read these compound words?

someday   birdhouse   watercolors
bedroom   somewhere   bluebird

Tell what words each compound word is made from.

Try This

Help your teacher make a list of other compound words on the chalkboard.

City Friends

The Sidewalk Is My Yard

The sidewalk is my yard,
The lamp post is my tree.
Up three long flights of stairs,
My home is marked 4 C.

The fire escape my porch,
Where clothes hang out to dry.
All day the noise and rush,
All night the trains go by.

Tall buildings all around
Reach up and shadow me.
Sometimes the great big sun
Comes peeping round to see.

All day the people pass,
They hurry as they go.
But when they are my friends,
They stop and say Hello.

LOIS LENSKI

A Baby in the House

It was a cold, winter afternoon.
The snow that fell was mixed with
rain, and so Pat stayed in the house.
When a car came up the street,
Pat jumped up and looked out.
But it was not his father's car.

"He will come home before long,"
said the woman who sat with Pat.
"When he comes, he will tell you."

It was dark when Father came home.
He went to Pat and picked him up.
"Pat, old boy, I have a surprise
for you!" said Father.

"Is it a boy?" asked Pat.

"No, a girl!" said Father.
"We have a little baby girl.
Her name is Pam."

A girl! That was something for Pat
to think about.
He had wished and wished for a boy.
Just thinking about a baby girl
made him mad.

In four days, Pat's mother came home with the baby.

On that day, Pat and his friend played together in the snow.

"You look mad," said Pat's friend.

"I am mad," said Pat.
"Mom came home with the baby this morning.
Who needs a baby girl around?"

"Oh, a baby girl is not so bad!" said the friend.
"All I have is a dog."

"I wish I had a dog," said Pat.
"I'll trade the baby for your dog."

"You can't do that," said Pat's friend.
"But I'll tell you what.
You can live at my house so you
won't have to stay around her."

"Good," Pat said as he began to run.
"I'll go home and get my things."

When Pat got home, his mother
was in the kitchen.
She was mixing milk for the baby.
In the next room, the baby cried.

Pat walked over to his mother.

He was all set to tell her that he was moving out of the house.

But then he stopped.

"Mom will get mad," he said to himself.

Just then a man rapped on the door.

As Pat's mother went to the back door, the baby cried and cried.

Pat went to the door of the baby's room.

He looked at the little baby.

"She is so little," he said to himself.

Pat put his hand on the baby.
She looked up at Pat.
Before long she stopped crying.

Soon Pat's mother came in.
"Pat, you are magic!" she said.
"You made her stop crying.
What did you do?"

"She likes me," said Pat in surprise.

"Do you like her?" asked Mother.

"She is not so bad," said Pat.
And away he ran to tell his friend.

Lester's Tomorrow

Lester's things were all over his room.
He was in his room when his mother
came to the door.

"Lester, what were you doing all
day?" she said.
"Your things are all over the room.
Pick them up and put them away."

Lester looked around.
"What things, Mom?"

"What things?" said his mother.
"I see six toys you have not put away.
Look at that box of rocks.
And what about the bag of shells?
Your mouse cage is on the chair.
Your bird's nest is under your bed.
Just look at that jar of frog eggs.
And pull your sheets up on your bed."

"But, Mom," said Lester, "I just got
a sheet of paper to write to Dad.
I can work on my room tomorrow."

After school the next day, Lester
went to work.

He picked up four books to put away.

But then he lay down on his bed
and opened the book on top.

It was about the moon and stars.

The next book that Lester opened
was about spiders and bugs.

The last two he opened were just
as good as the first two.

Soon the afternoon was over.

"I can work on this old room
tomorrow," said Lester to himself.

When tomorrow came, Lester came
home from school and went to work.

He looked at his jar of frog eggs.

It needed water, and Lester got some.

Then he opened the mouse cage.

He took out his little pet mouse
and opened a box of seeds.

He put some seeds in his hand.

The mouse sniffed at Lester's hand.

Then it sniffed the seeds and took
some of them.

After that, Lester and the mouse
played on the bed.

When the afternoon was over, Lester's things were still all over his room.

His mother came to his door.

She looked mad, and Lester had to think fast.

"Mom, I had to look after my mouse. I'll work tomorrow," he said.

The next day was not a school day.

Lester said, "I can't work this morning after all.

Did you forget, Mom?

This is the day of the big party.

All the children are going."

"I'll tell you about one boy who is not going," said Lester's mother.

"That boy is going to stay home and put his things away."

"No, Mom, no!" cried Lester.
"I'll do it the first thing tomorrow."

"Not tomorrow, but now!" said Mom.

Lester was sad, but he got to work.
His tomorrow had come!

Lost in the Big City

Carla and her mother had just come from a dress shop.

They had two big shopping bags.

They had shopped all day, and now they were going home.

They were in line at the bus stop with many other people.

The bus came down the street
and stopped.

Carla took her mother's hand, and
they got on the bus.

Many people were on the bus, and so
Carla and her mother did not sit down.

The bus made many stops.

Some people got out, but many other
people got in.

As the people went to the back of the
bus, Carla let go of her mother's hand.

Before long, Carla was in the back of
the bus.

Carla looked around, but she did not see her mother.

Soon she began to think that her mother was not on the bus at all!

But just then, Carla saw a woman who had her back to her.

"That must be Mom," said Carla.

"Mom has on a dark dress like that."

The woman got out at the next stop. Carla jumped out after her.

"Mom!" she yelled.

"Did you forget about me?"

When the woman looked around, Carla saw that she was not her mother.

"Oh! Where is Mother?" asked Carla as the woman walked away.

Just then, a policeman saw Carla. He walked over to her.

"Are you lost, little girl?" asked the policeman.

"No, I'm not lost," said Carla. "But my mother is."

"Who is your mother?" asked the policeman.

Carla said, "Her name is Mom, and I'm Carla."

"Where do you live?" asked the policeman.

"We live in a tall building," said Carla.

The policeman opened the door of
a green box.

Then he said something into the box.

"I have a lost girl," he said.

"Her name is Carla, but she is too
little to tell where she lives."

"Oh, no!" said Carla. "I can't be lost.
I am with you. My mother is lost."

"Where do you think your mother is?" asked the policeman.

"On the bus," said Carla.

The policeman took Carla's hand.
They went down the street together.

Soon a car pulled over and stopped.
Carla's father jumped out.
"Carla! Carla!" he yelled.

"Dad!" cried Carla. "Mom is lost!"

"Is she?" asked Carla's father.
"What a funny Mom! She came home and said you were lost!"

The New Girl in School

It was going to be Jan's first day
in a new school.

"Mom," she said, "can't I go back
to my old school?"

"Your old school is too far away,"
Jan's mother said.
"But you will like your new school.
You will soon make many
new friends."

But Jan still wished she were back in
her old school with her old friends.

Jan held her mother's hand as she
went into her new school.

The two of them went together
to the door of the new room.

Then Jan's mother went back home.

The new room did not look like
Jan's room in the old school.

The teacher was new to her.

The books were new to her, too.
So was the work.

The teacher asked Jan to tell the
children about her old school.

But Jan just sat.

The children began to work, but Jan still just sat.

She did not do a thing all morning.

When the morning was over, the children got in a line.

Then they went to the lunch room.

Jan sat next to the teacher in the lunch room.

After lunch, the boys and girls played together out in the yard.

But Jan did not go out to play.

She just sat in the lunch room.

Soon she began to cry.

A boy came and saw Jan crying.
He ran back to the other children.

"That new girl must be a cry baby,"
said the boy.
"She is crying in the lunch room."

"What is she crying about?"
asked a girl.

"She won't tell," said the boy.

"Penny can tell you," said the teacher.
"Don't forget she was a new girl.
She cried, too, on her first day.
I think she can get Jan to come out."

Penny ran into the lunch room,
and soon came out with Jan.

The two girls held hands as they
came running down the walk.

"Jan is all right now," said Penny.

"Let her play with us," said a girl.

"She will play with you tomorrow and
the next day," said Penny.

"Right now, we are just going to play
together. Jan is my friend first."

My Friend Pete

Pete is the name of my best friend.
I met Pete when I was a little boy.
Now I am big and I go to school.

Pete is in my room at school.
I sit next to Pete when the
teacher lets me.

Pete and I walk to school together.
We sit together at lunch.
We play together in the school yard.
After school, we walk home together.

I like to sleep at Pete's house.
He likes to sleep at my house, too.
When we do that, we do not go
to sleep right away.
We put out the lights and look at
the moon and stars.
Then Pete tells me funny things.
And I tell funny things to him.

I can't forget the day that Pete
got mad at me.

I was in his room, and he was
in the yard.

All I was going to do was play
with his pet bird.

But when I took down the cage, the
door came open, and the bird got out.

It went around and around his room.

I ran after it, but the bird was
too fast for me.

Next it went into the kitchen and
sat on the kitchen sink.

I ran over to the sink, but the bird
got away.

I had to get Pete.
I opened the door and yelled to him.
When I did that, out went the bird!

Pete saw the bird as it came out
the kitchen door.
He saw it go to the top of a tree.
Pete was so mad he saw red.

I ran home as fast as lightning.
It was a good thing that Pete
did not come after me.

Doing Something About It

After I got home all I did was think about Pete's bird.

I wished I had not opened the door of the bird cage.

I wished I had not made Pete mad.

It was Mom who helped me see
what I had to do.

Mom is good at things like that.

She said I had to think of something
good to do for Pete.

I went to my room and sat down
on my bed.

Then I did the best thinking a
little boy can do.

At last I had it!

In my room, I had a small green turtle in a dish.

I took the turtle out of its dish.
I held my pet in my hand.

"You are the best turtle in the world," I said.

"But from now on you must be Pete's turtle.

He likes you, too.
You will help him forget his bird."

I held the turtle in my hand, and together we went to Pete's house.

When I got to Pete's house, I saw his bird in a small tree.

It was looking right at me.

I ran to the house, got the cage, and put it in the yard.

Then I hid in back of a log with my turtle still in my hand.

The bird came to the cage and hopped right into it.

I jumped fast, got the cage, and took it to Pete's room.

Boy, was I happy to have that
bird back!

I got it some water and bird seed.
That bird was hungry, all right.

At last Pete came in.
The first thing he saw was his bird.
Then he saw me.
He got over being mad right away.

"THANKS!" he said. "THANK YOU!"

I had three things to make me happy.
Pete had his bird back.
I still had my turtle.
And best of all, Pete was still
my best friend.

Can You Read This?

Carla was going fishing.

She got her fishing rod and went down to the river.

When she got to the river bank, Carla put her fishing line into the water.

Then she sat very still.

Soon something pulled on Carla's line.

Carla jumped up!

She pulled her line from the water.

"I had no luck at all," said Carla.

"But I'll bet the next one won't get away."

167

Thinking Back

What is the best name for the story?

The River Bank

The Fish That Got Away

Carla's Good Luck

New Ways with Words

Can you read these words from the story?

rod   river   bank

luck   bet

Look at the words below.

fish   fishing   fished   fishes

What word do you find in all of them?
Fish is called the **root word**.

Try This

Find the root word in each set.

asking   brightly   dancing

asked   brighten   danced

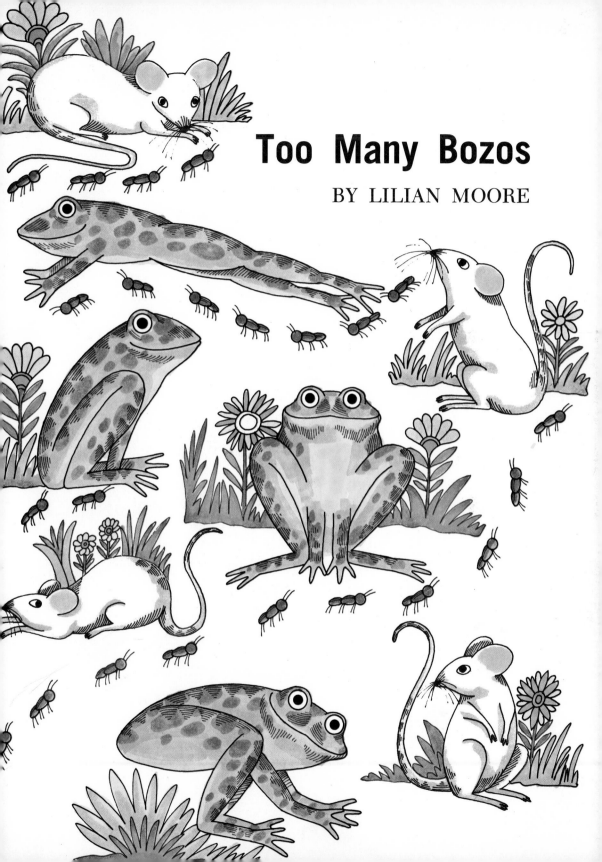

Too Many Bozos

BY LILIAN MOORE

In the Park

"Mother," said Danny Drake, "can I have a dog?"

Danny's mother looked at Danny.
"Danny Drake," she said, "you asked me that this morning.
And what did I tell you?"

"No," said Danny.

"You asked me that on other days," said his mother.
"And what did I tell you then?"

"No," said Danny.

Danny's mother said, "No, Danny!
This house is too small for a dog."

"But I have a good name for a dog,"
said Danny.
"I can name him Bozo."

"NO, Danny!" said his mother.

And so that was that.

Danny ran out to the park to play.
He played with his friend Pete.
They played together all afternoon.

"Look," said Pete as he pulled
his hat down over his ears.
"I'm a robber."

"Then where is your mask?"
asked Danny.

"I don't need a mask," Pete said as he
hid in back of a big rock at the pond.

"I'll be a policeman," said Danny
to himself.
"I'll go after the robber."

As Danny came to the rock, a little
green frog jumped up.

Danny saw the little frog before Pete.
And Danny just had to have
that frog for a pet.
Pete helped Danny get the frog.
They picked up a box and put the
frog in it.
Then Danny took the frog home.

"Oh, boy!" Danny said to the frog.
"Am I happy I saw you.
Won't Mom be surprised!"

Bozo the Frog

Danny went to tell his mother
about the frog.
He hid it in back of him.

"Mom," he said, "Are <u>you</u> going to be
surprised when you see what I have!"

Danny held up the frog.
Mom <u>was</u> surprised.

"Now I have a pet," Danny said to his mother.

"Do you wish to pet him?"

"No, thanks," said Danny's mother.

"I'm going to name my pet Bozo," Danny said.

"Bozo. Bozo the Frog."

"Then tell Bozo the Frog to stay in <u>your</u> room," said Danny's mother.

Danny put Bozo the Frog in his
room and looked after him.

He made a good home for him and
took him things to eat.

What fun the frog was!
And what big jumps he made!

First Danny put down one book.
Bozo jumped right over it.
Then Danny put down two books,
then three.

And Bozo jumped over them all.

But one day Bozo made one jump
too many.

The door to his house was open.

Jump! Bozo was out of his house.
Jump! Jump! Bozo was out of
Danny's room.
Jump! Jump! Jump! Bozo was
all over the house.

At last Bozo came to the best
thing of all.

It was something with water in it,
and so Bozo jumped right into it.

He was in the kitchen sink.

The sink was filled with dishes.

Bozo sat on Mom's best green dish.

Soon Danny's mother came in
to do the dishes.

She let out a big yell when she
saw Bozo.

Poor Bozo was so mixed up he
jumped out of the sink.

He jumped right at Danny's mother!

"A frog in my sink! Oh, no!"
Danny's mother cried.

"Danny, get that frog out of this
house right away."

Danny was very sad when he
put Bozo into the box.

He was very sad as he walked
back to the park.

180

On the street to the park, Danny
met his friend Billy.

"Look what I have," said Billy.
He held up a little cage.

"Look what I have," said Danny.
He opened the box just a little.

Right then, the boys made a trade.
Billy took the box and Danny took
the cage.

Bozo the Mouse

Danny raced back to his home.
"Oh, boy," he said to himself.
"Am I happy I met Billy.
Won't Mom be surprised when
she sees what I have now!"

Mom <u>was</u> surprised!
Danny held up the cage for her
to see.
In the cage was a little mouse.

"This is my new pet," Danny said
to his mother.
"I'm going to name him Bozo.
Bozo the Mouse."

Danny took the mouse from the cage.
"Look, Mom," he said.
"I'll let you pet him."

"No, thanks," said Danny's mother.
"And Danny Drake, don't let that
mouse out of your room."

"It's all right, Mom," said Danny.
"Bozo the Mouse won't get in the
kitchen sink."

Danny put Bozo the Mouse in his
room and looked after him.

He made things for the cage.

He put things to eat and drink in it.

He played with Bozo day after day.

Bozo the Mouse did not get into
the kitchen sink.

But the morning came when Bozo
got out of his cage.

He got out of Danny's room.

And he went right to the kitchen.

Sniff, sniff, went Bozo the Mouse.
Something good was in the kitchen.

Danny's mother had just made
a cake for a party.
That is, it <u>was</u> for a party before
Bozo the Mouse began to eat it.

Danny's mother took a good look
at her cake.

"My cake!" she cried. "Now what
will we eat at the party?"

Then she said, "Danny Drake!
Get that cake-eating mouse out of
the house right away."

Danny was sad when he put the
mouse into his cage.

"The best home for Bozo the Mouse
is back at the pet shop," he said.

"After all, that is where Billy got
the mouse."

So Danny took Bozo to the pet shop.

The Best Bozo of All

The pet shop man was happy to
get the little mouse back.
He and Danny made a trade.

Danny ran home like a flash.
"Oh, boy!" he said to himself.
"Am I happy I went to the pet shop!
What will Mom think when she
sees what I have now!"

At first, Danny's mother just looked
at the box.
Then she asked, "What in the world
is that, Danny?"

Danny held up the box.
"This is my ant farm," Danny said.
"See all the ants?
I like to see them work."

"Ants!" cried Danny's mother.
"I'll have ants all over the house.
No ants, Danny Drake.
Ants can't stay in this house."

"But, Mother," said Danny.
"I just <u>have</u> to have a pet."

"Yes," said Danny's mother. "I can see that you do.

I can think of just the pet for you," she said.

"You can?" said Danny. "Is it as good as a frog?"

"Oh, yes," said his mother.

"Is it as good as a mouse?" asked Danny.

"I think it is," said his mother.

"Is it as good as the ant farm?" asked Danny.

"Oh, yes," said his mother. "It is the best pet in all the world.

Danny Drake, you can have a dog for a pet."

"A DOG," cried Danny. "A DOG!"

"A little dog," said Danny's mother. "This house is little, and so it has to be a little dog."

"Oh, boy!" said Danny, "a dog!
What do you think I'm going to name
him? Bozo. Bozo the Dog."

"Bozo," said Danny's mother.
"What a surprise!"